JOHN THOMPSON'S EASIEST PIANO COURSE

PIANO POPS

Apologize 26

Bridge Over Troubled Water 10

Clocks 24

Close To You (They Long To Be) 14

Don't Know Why 20

Everytime 8

Imagine 2

Lean On Me 12

Mad World 6

Piano Man 18

Run 28

Someone Like You 16

Take A Bow 22

We Belong Together 4

Your Song 30

This collection of popular piano songs is intended as supplementary material for those working through **John Thompson's Easiest Piano Course** Parts 2–4. The pieces may also be used for sight reading practice by more advanced students.

Dynamics and phrasing have been deliberately omitted from the earlier pieces, since they are not introduced until Part 3 of the Easiest Piano Course, and initially the student's attention should be focused on playing notes and rhythms accurately. Outline fingering has been included, and in general the hand is assumed to remain in a five-finger position until a new fingering indicates a position shift. The fingering should suit most hands, although logical alternatives are always possible.

Imagine

Words & Music by John Lennon

Moderately

I-mag-ine there's no heav-en; it's ea-sy if you try. No hell be-low us; a-bove us on-ly sky. I-mag-ine all the peo-ple,

© Copyright 1971 Lenono Music.
All Rights Reserved. International Copyright Secured.

11
liv - ing for to - day.
You may say I'm a dream - er,
3
15
but I'm not the on - ly one.
I hope some day you'll
1
3 1 2 1
18
join us,
and the world will live as one.

We Belong Together

Words & Music by Mariah Carey, Jermaine Dupri, Kenneth Edmonds, Manuel Seal, Bobby Womack, Darnell Bristol, Sidney Johnson, Johnta Austin, Patrick Moten & Sandra Sully

Strongly

The feel-ing that I'm feel-ing now that I don't hear your voice,

or have your touch and kiss your lips, 'cause I don't have a choice.

Oh, what I would-n't give to have you ly-ing by my side, right here. 'Cause

© Copyright 2005 ECAF Music/Rye Songs/Warner-Tamerlane Publishing Corporation/Slack Ad Music/Naked Under My Clothes Music/Shaniah Cymone Music/Sony ATV Songs LLC , USA.
Sony/ATV Music Publishing/ABKCO Music Limited/Universal/MCA Music Limited/Universal Music Publishing MGB Limited/Chrysalis Music Limited/EMI Music Publishing Limited/Copyright Control.
All Rights Reserved. International Copyright Secured.

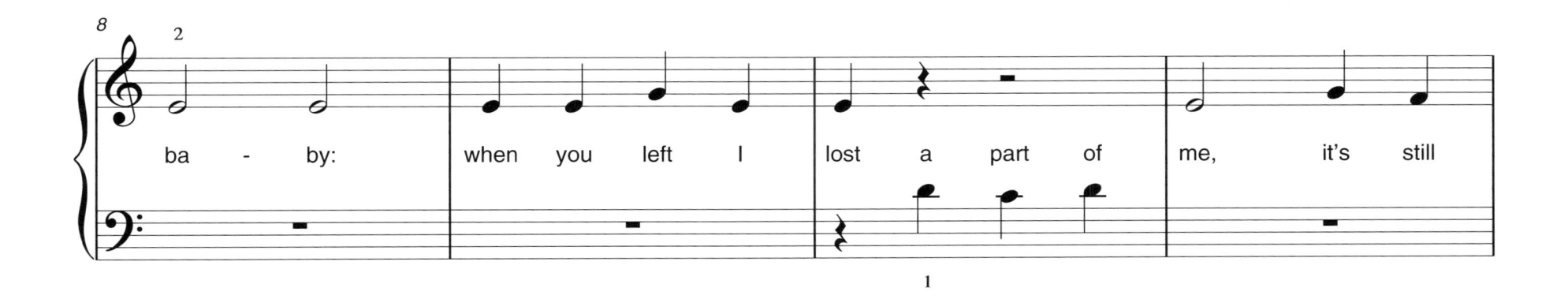

ba - by: when you left I lost a part of me, it's still so hard to be - lieve. Come back ba - by, please, 'cause we be - long to - geth - er, we be - long to - geth - er.

Mad World

Words & Music by Roland Orzabal

Darkly

All a-round me are fam-i-liar fa-ces, worn out pla-ces, worn out fa-ces. Bright and ear-ly for their dai-ly ra-ces, go-ing no-where, go-ing no-where. And I find it kind of fun - ny, I find it kind of sad, that dreams in which I'm dy - ing are the best I've ev - er had. I find it hard to tell you, I find it hard to take, when peo - ple run in cir - cles, it's a ver - y, ver - y mad world, mad world.

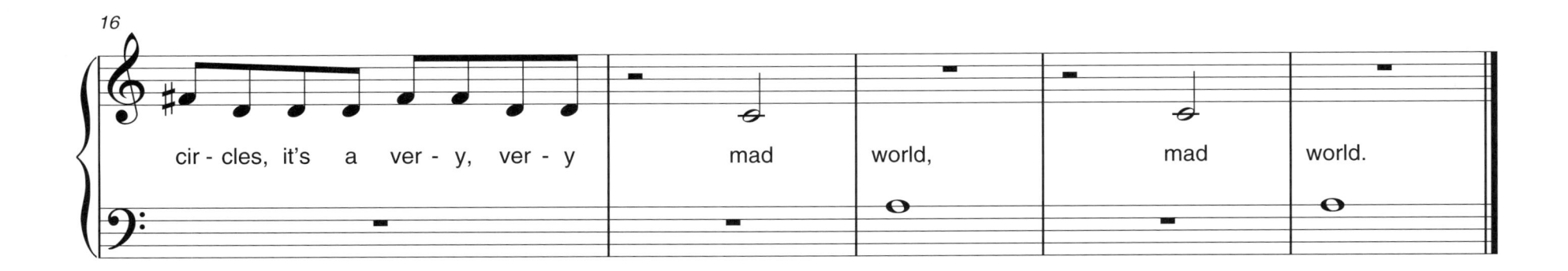

Everytime

Words & Music by Britney Spears & Annette Stamatelatos

Warmly

No - tice me, take my hand.

Why are we stran - gers when our love is

strong? Why car - ry on with - out me? Ev - 'ry time I

© Copyright 2003 Britney Spears Music/Imagem Music/Notting Hill Music (UK) Limited/Universal Music Publishing Limited.
All Rights Reserved. International Copyright Secured.

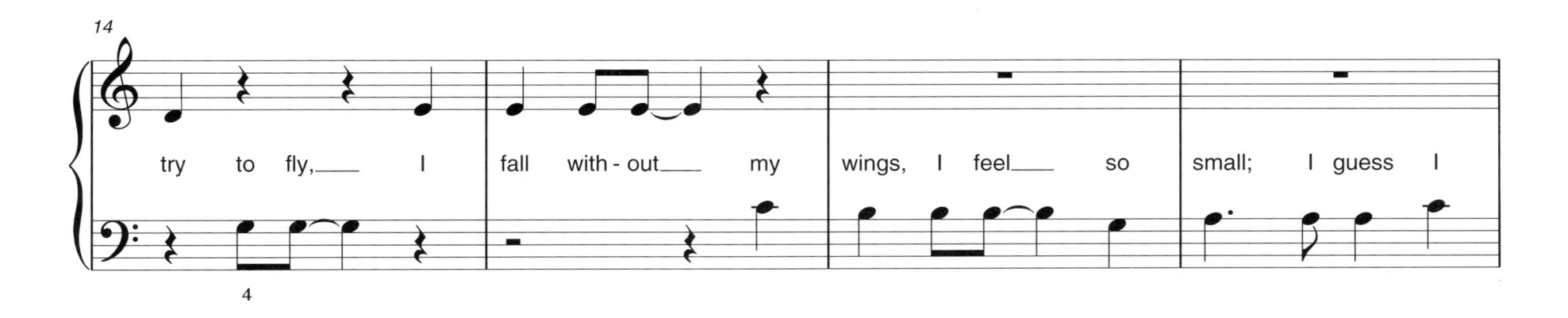

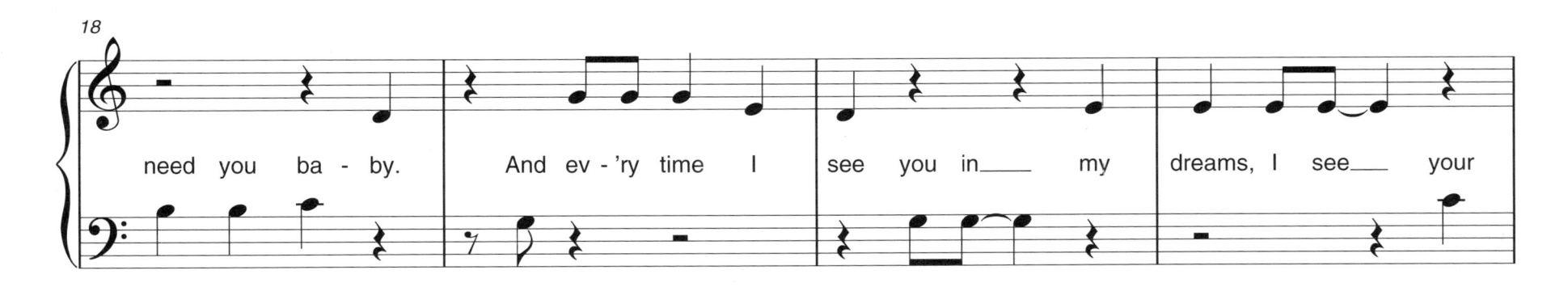

try to fly,___ I fall with-out___ my wings, I feel___ so small; I guess I need you ba-by. And ev-'ry time I see you in___ my dreams, I see___ your face, it's haunt-ing me; I guess I need you ba-by.

Bridge Over Troubled Water

Words & Music by Paul Simon

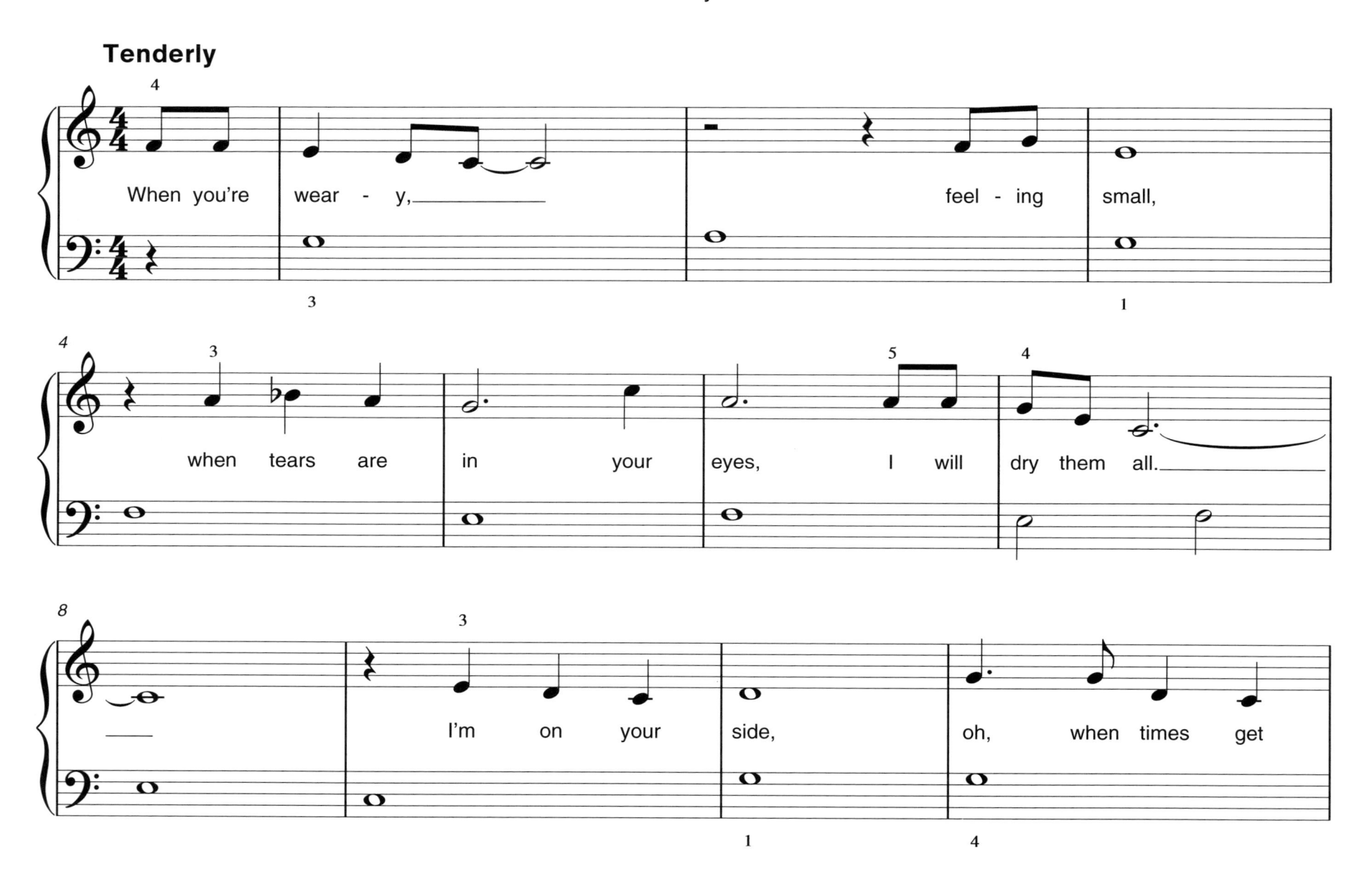

Tenderly

When you're wear-y, feel-ing small, when tears are in your eyes, I will dry them all. I'm on your side, oh, when times get

© Copyright 1969 Paul Simon (BMI).
All Rights Reserved. International Copyright Secured.

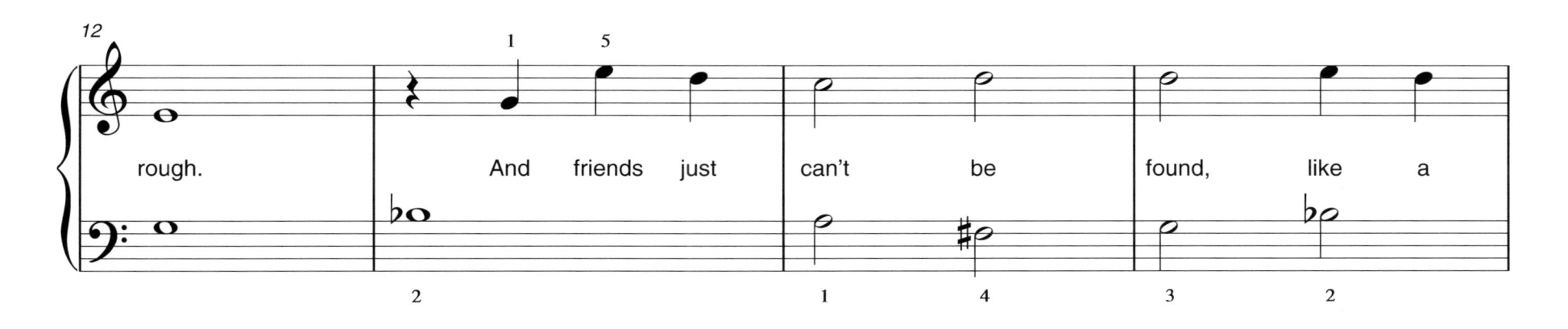

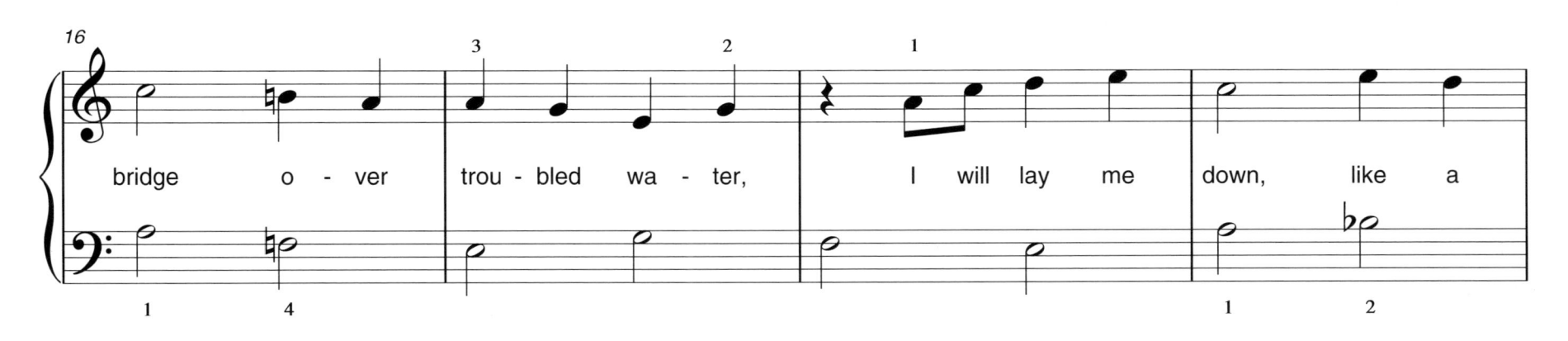

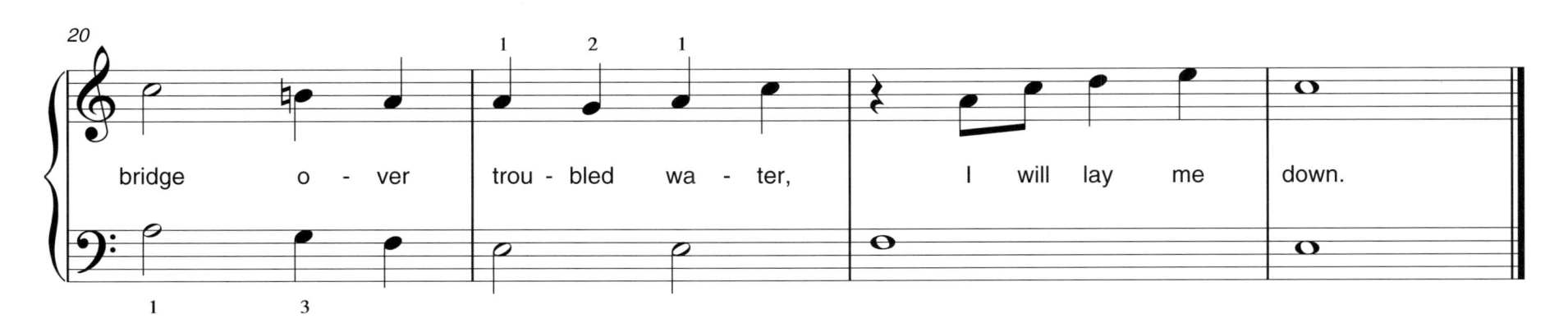

rough. And friends just can't be found, like a bridge o-ver trou-bled wa-ter, I will lay me down, like a bridge o-ver trou-bled wa-ter, I will lay me down.

Lean On Me

Words & Music by Bill Withers

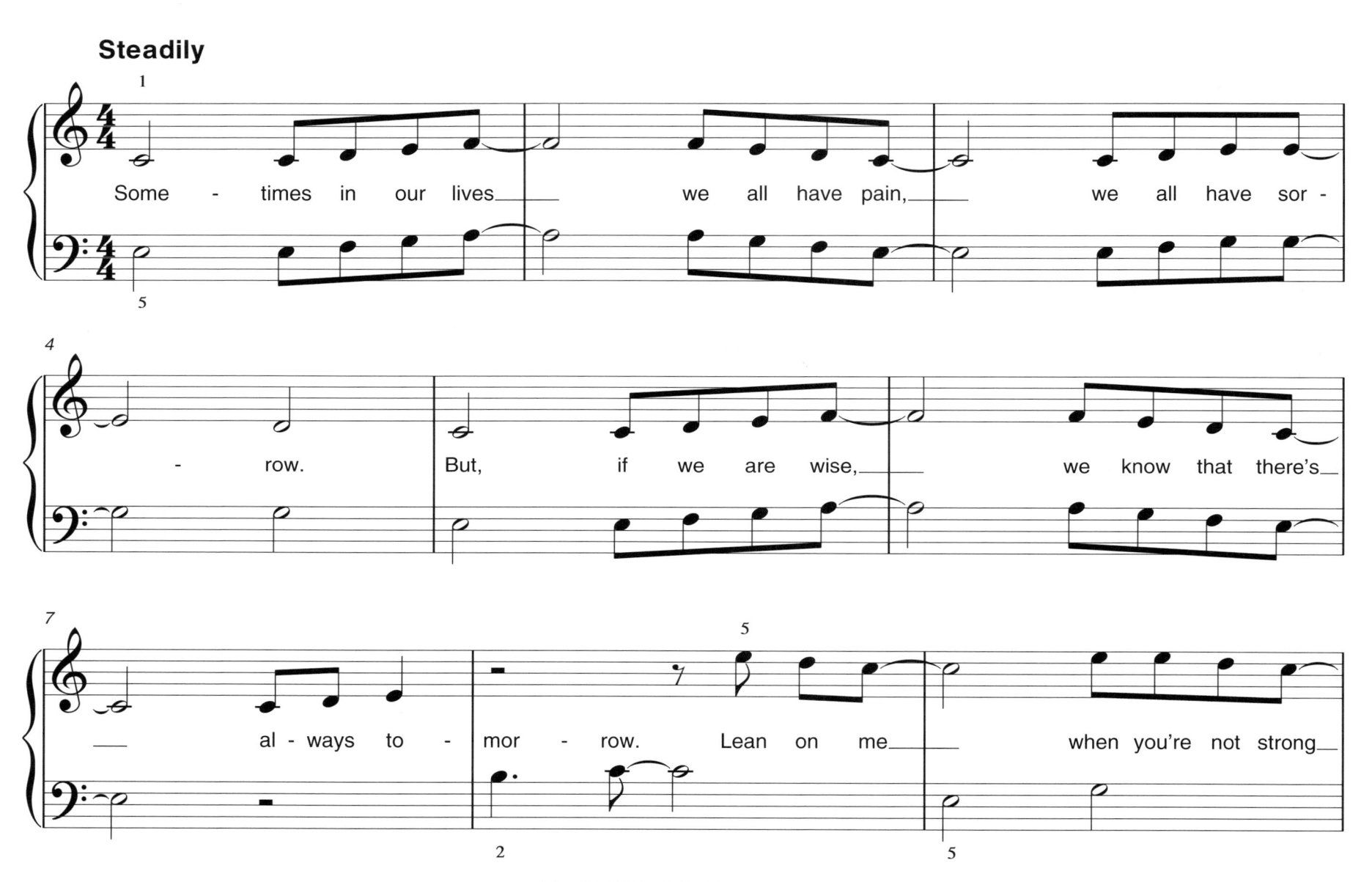

10
4
3
and I'll be your friend,
I'll help you car - ry on;
13
1 4
5
for, it won't be long
'til I'm gon - na need
some - bod - y to lean
16
5
1 2
on.
Call me,
call me,
call me,
call me.
2

Close To You (They Long To Be)

Words by Hal David & Music by Burt Bacharach

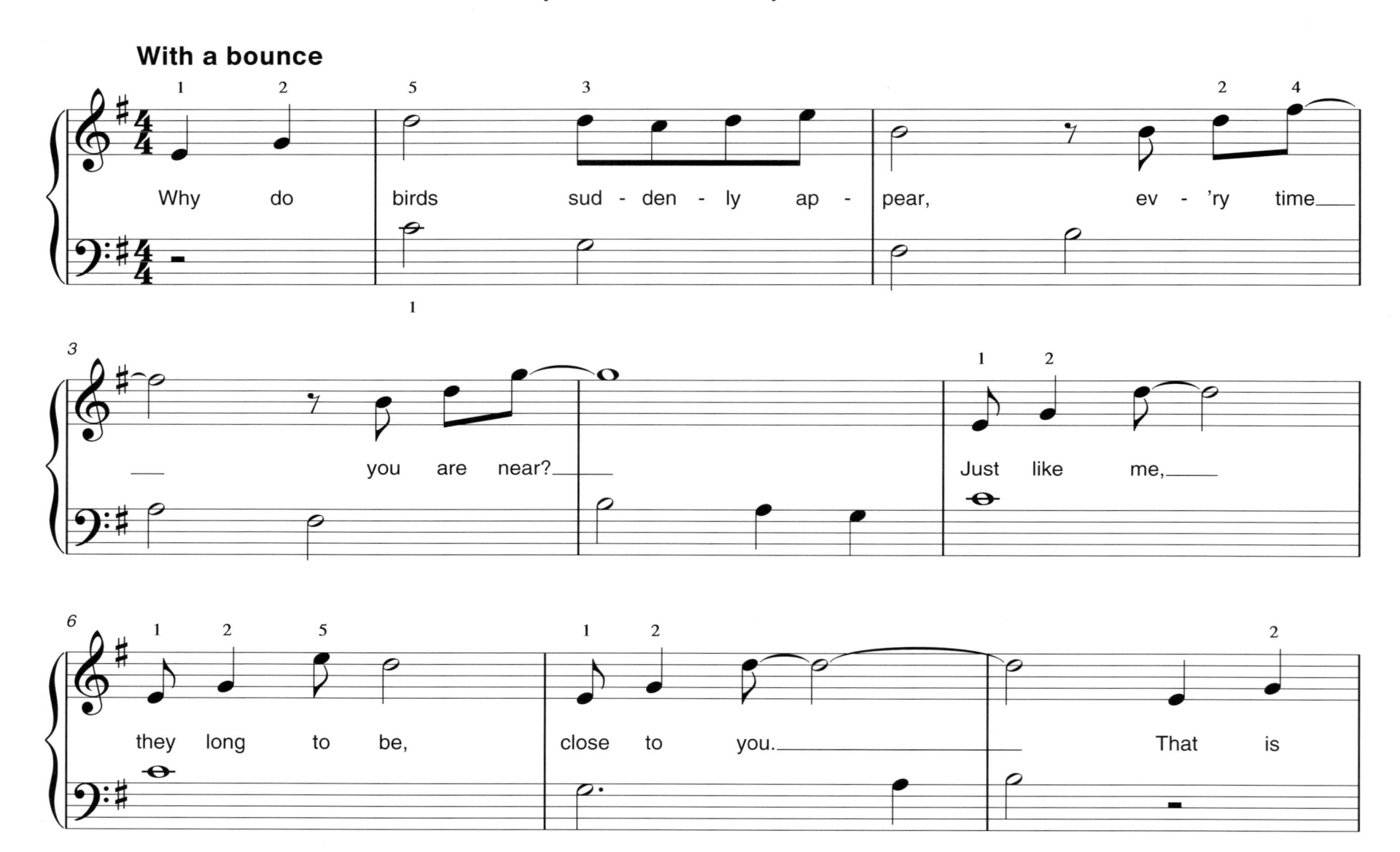

With a bounce

why all the girls in town fol-low you____ all a-round;____

just like me,____ they long to be, close to you.____

Just like me,____ they long to be, close to you.____

Someone Like You

Words & Music by Adele Adkins & Daniel Wilson

Strongly

f Nev-er mind,___ I'll find some-one like you - - -oo. I wish noth-ing but___ the best for you two. Don't for-get me, I begged; I'll___ re-

© Copyright 2010 Universal Music Publishing Limited/Sugar Lake Music/Chrysalis Music Limited.
All Rights Reserved. International Copyright Secured.

-mem - ber you said, "Some - times it lasts and loves, but some - times it hurts in - stead. Some - times it lasts and loves, but some - times it hurts in - stead."

17

Piano Man

Words & Music by Billy Joel

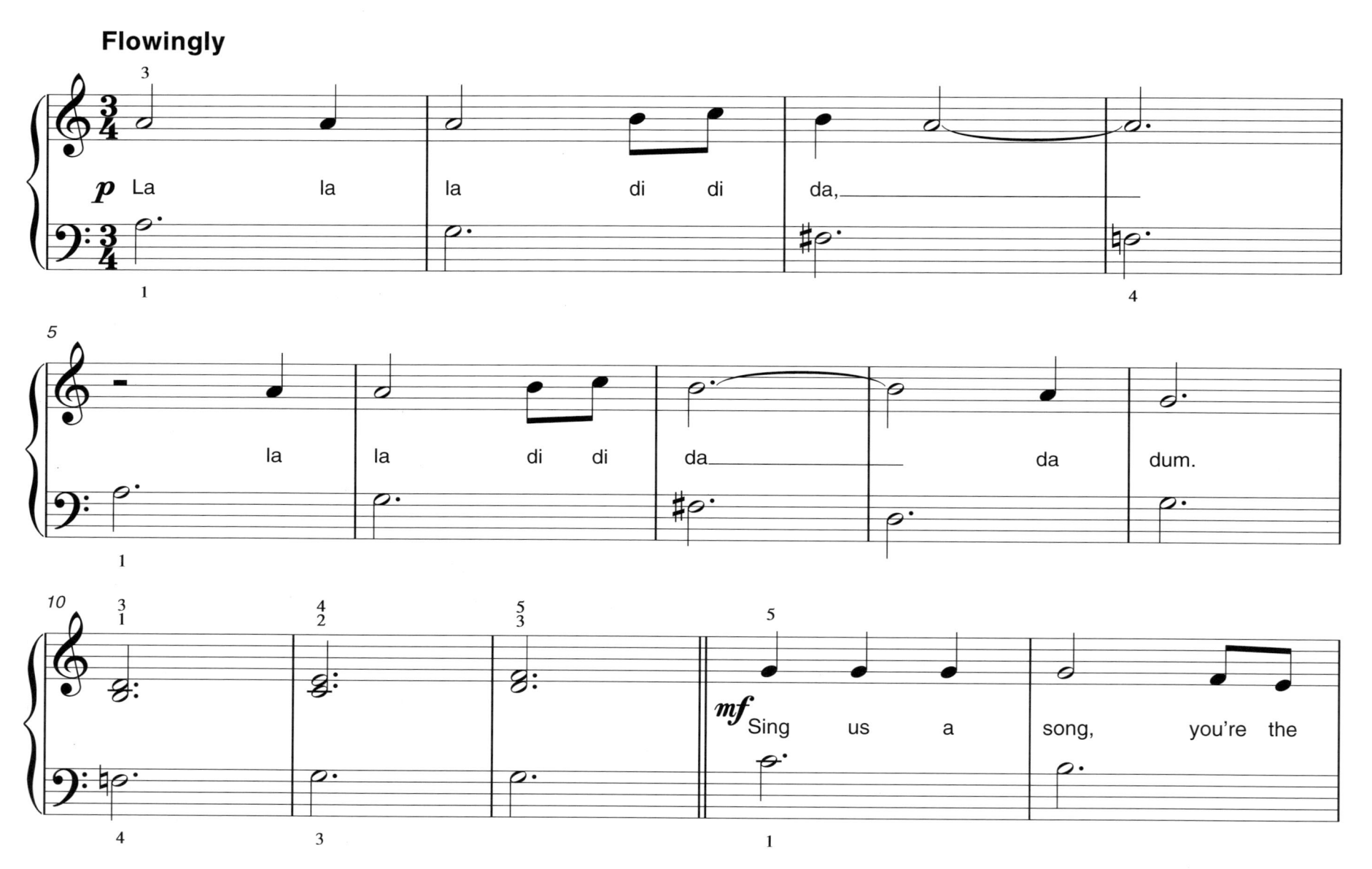

pia - no man; sing us a song to - night.

Well, we're all in the mood for a mel - o - dy,

and you've got us feel - in' al - right.

Don't Know Why

Words & Music by Jesse Harris

wine, _____ but you'll be on my mind for - ev - er.

mp Some - thing has _____ to make you run, _____ don't know why _____ I

did - n't come, don't know why _____ I did - n't come.

Take A Bow

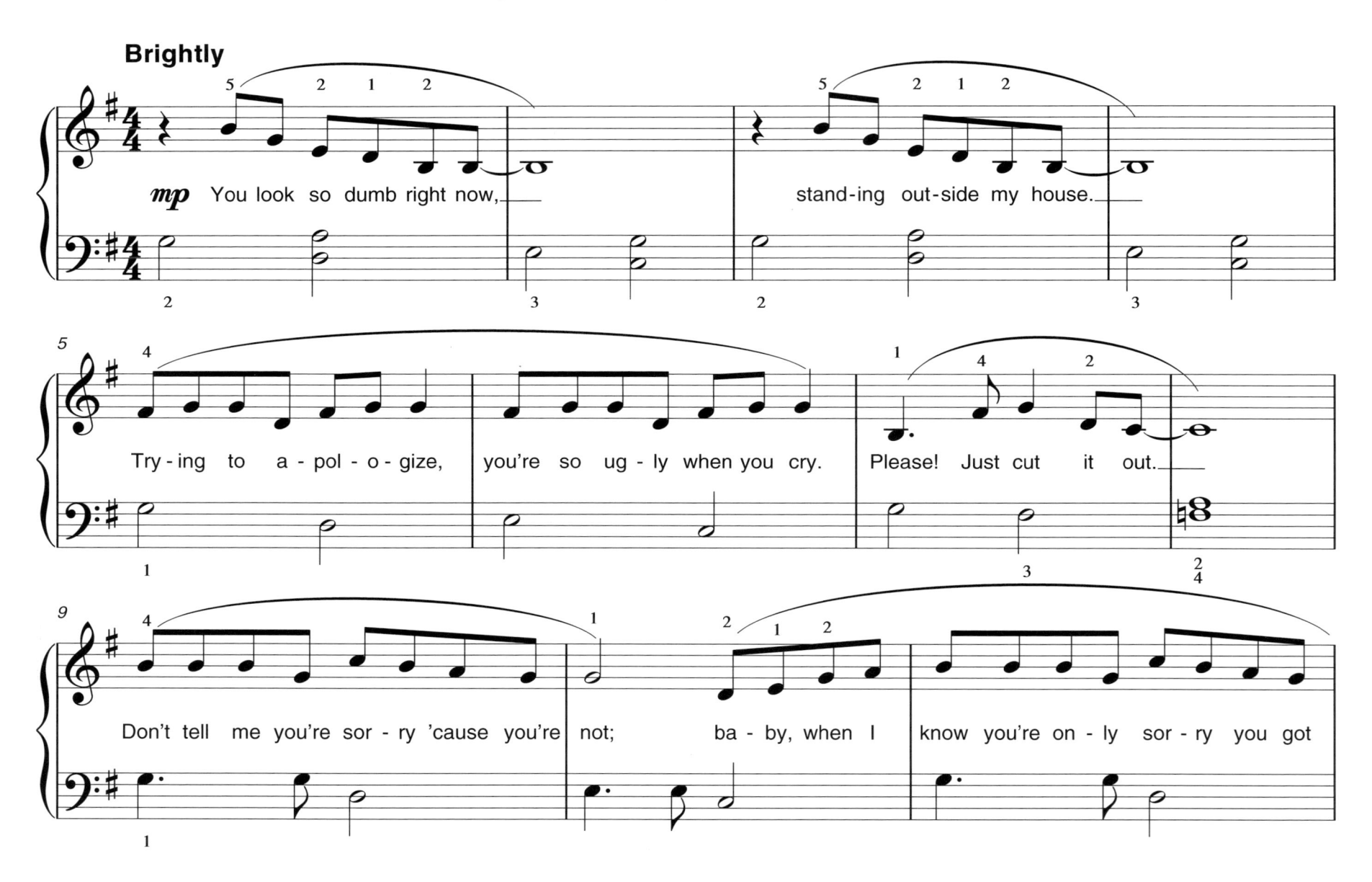

Words & Music by Mikkel Eriksen, Tor Erik Hermansen & Shaffer Smith

caught. But you put on quite a show, real-ly had me go-ing, but now it's time to go; cur-tain's fin-'ly clo-sing. That was quite a show, ver-y en-ter-tain-ing, but it's o-ver now;___ go on and take__ a bow.__ But it's o-ver now.___

Clocks

Words & Music by Guy Berryman, Chris Martin, Jon Buckland & Will Champion

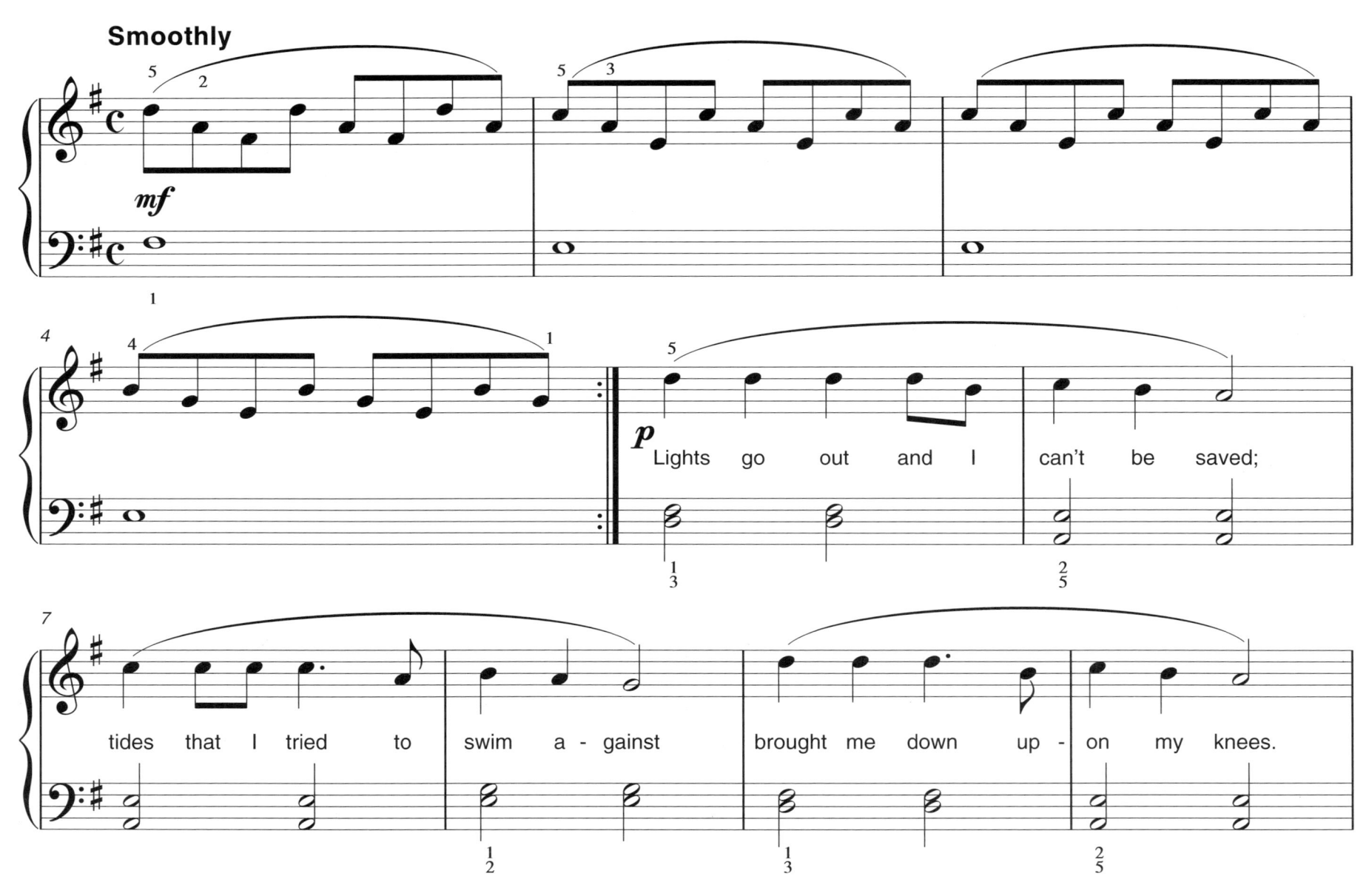

Smoothly

mf

p

Lights go out and I can't be saved; tides that I tried to swim a-gainst brought me down up-on my knees.

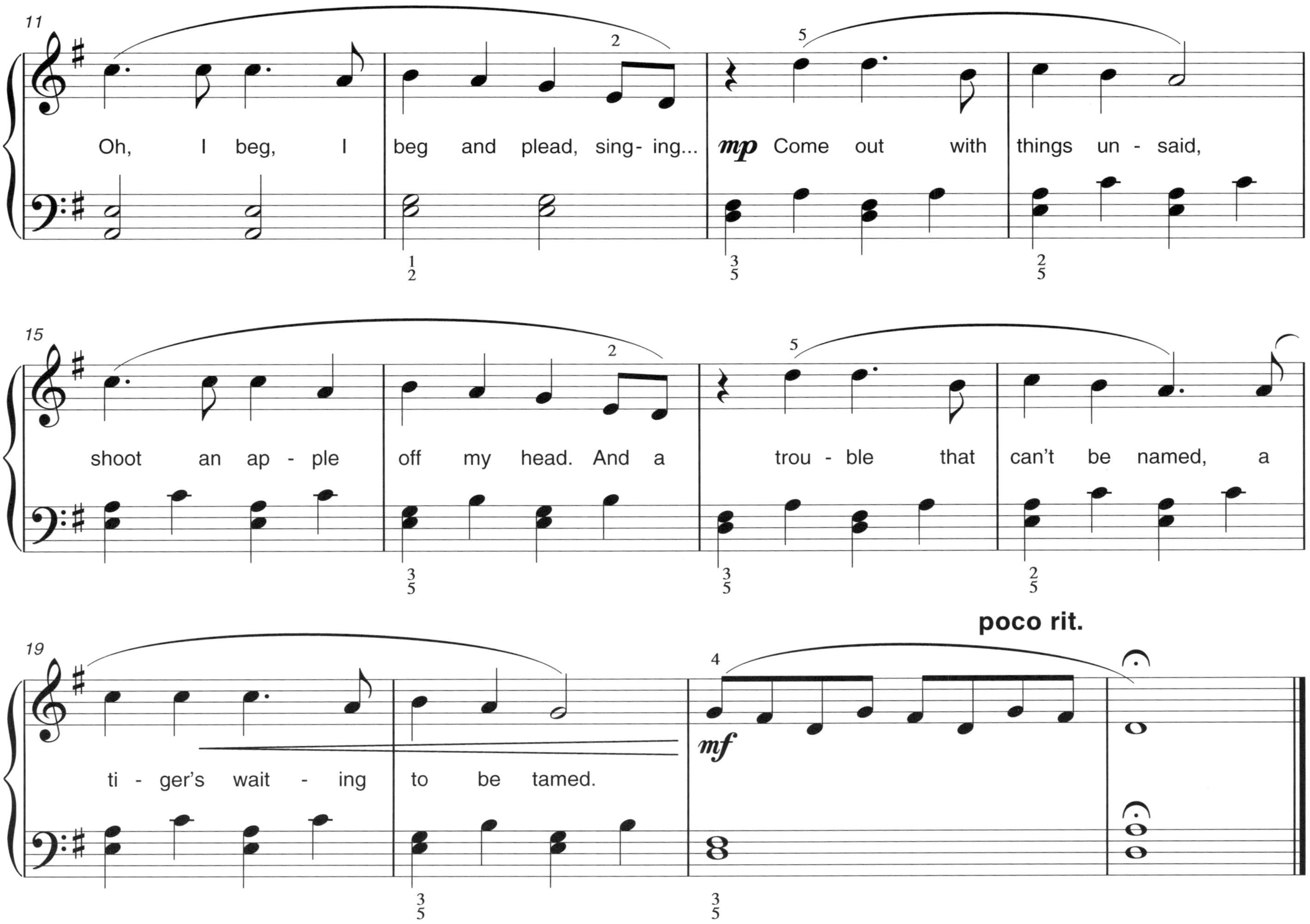

11
Oh, I beg, I beg and plead, sing- ing...
mp Come out with things un - said,
15
shoot an ap - ple off my head. And a
trou - ble that can't be named, a
19
ti - ger's wait - ing to be tamed.
poco rit.
mf

Apologize

Words & Music by Ryan Tedder

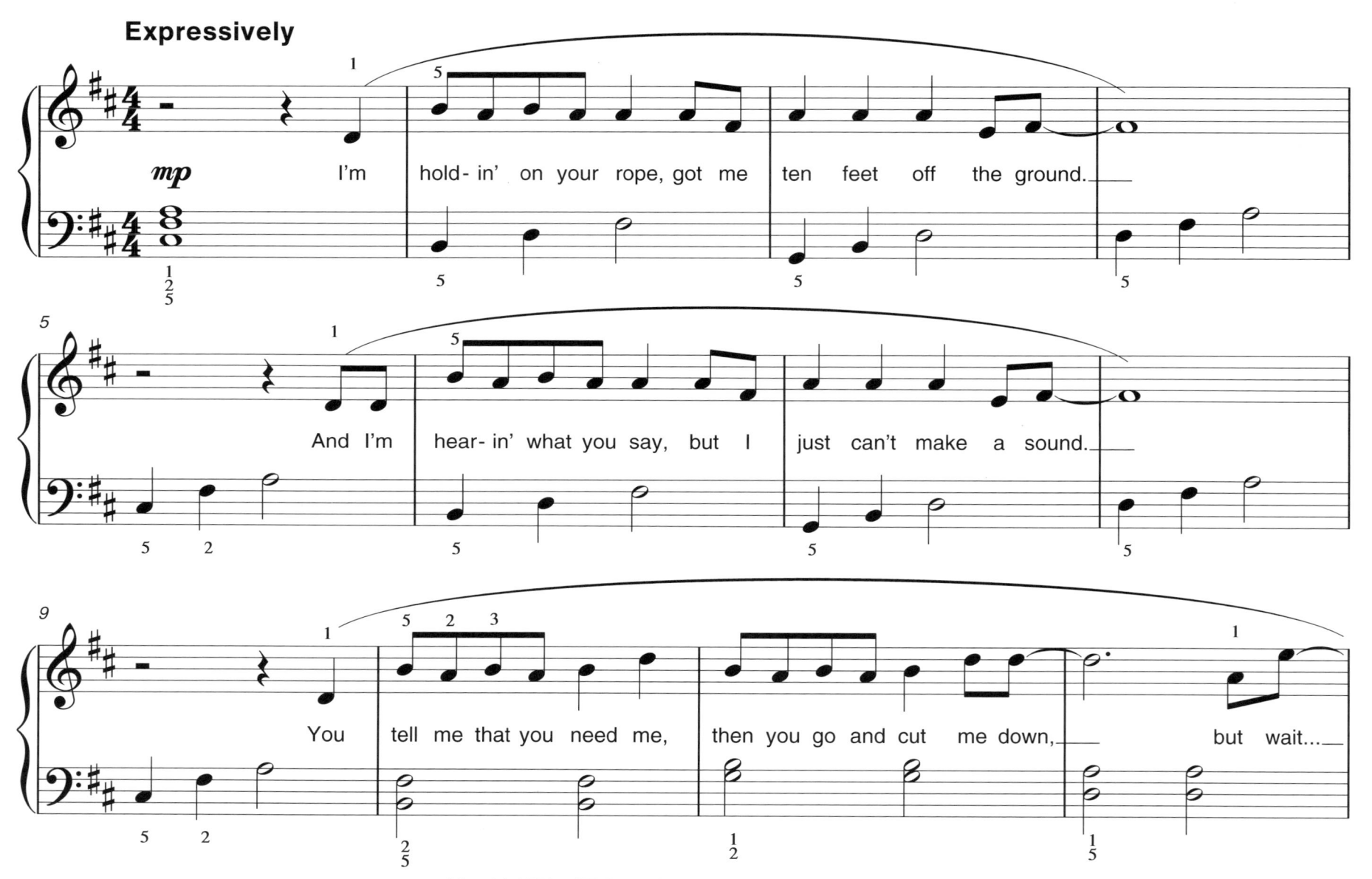

Expressively

13
You tell me that you're sor - ry, did - n't think I'd turn a - round and say...
17
that it's too late to 'pol - o - gize, it's too late. I said it's
f
22
too late to 'pol - o - gize, it's too late.
p

Run

Words & Music by Gary Lightbody, Jonathan Quinn, Mark McClelland, Nathan Connolly & Iain Archer

Softly

p I'll sing it one last time for you, then we real-ly have to go. You've been the on-ly thing that's right in all I've done.

f Light up, light up, as if you have a choice, e-ven if you can-not

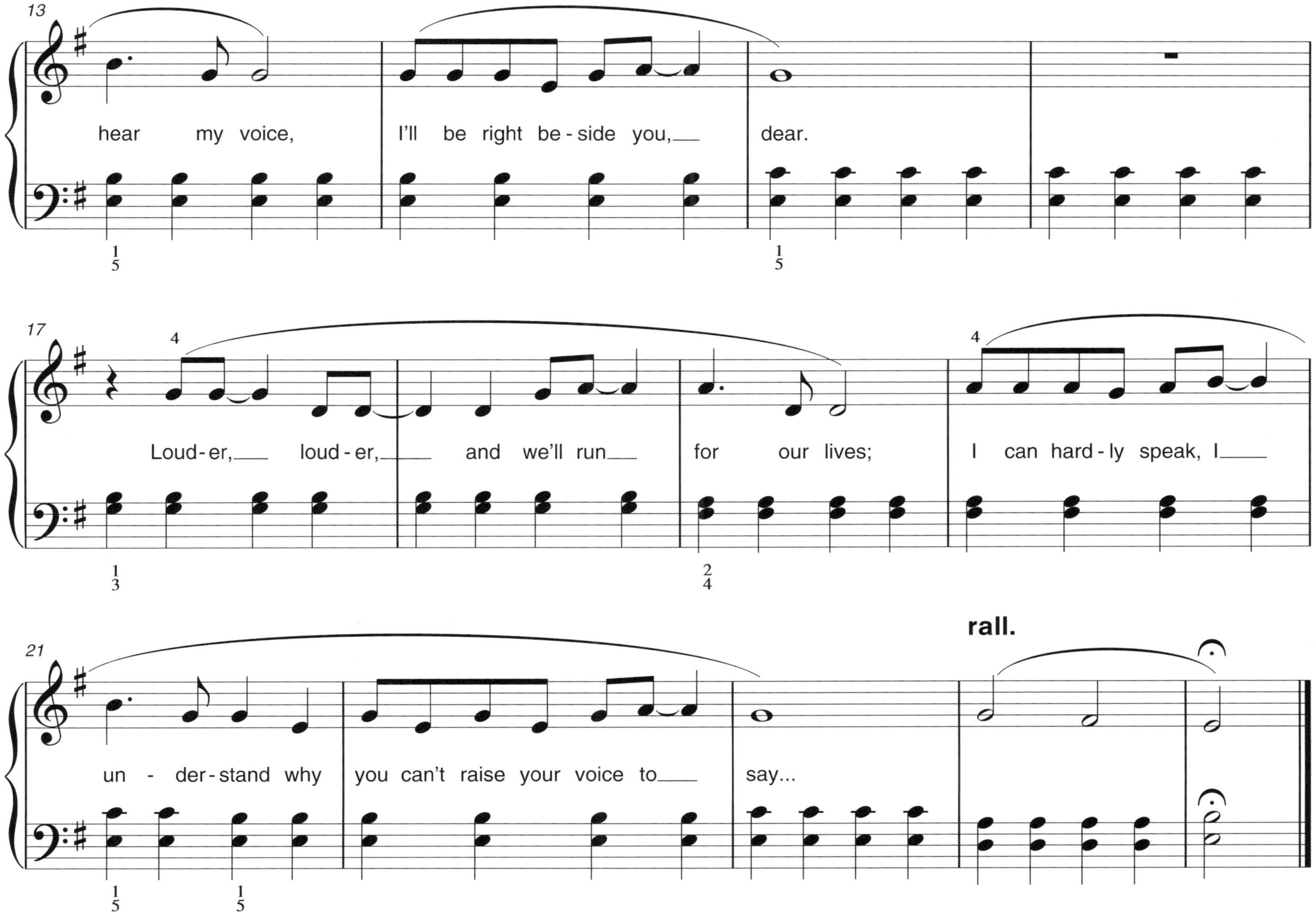
13
hear my voice, I'll be right be-side you,___ dear.
17
Loud-er,___ loud-er,___ and we'll run___ for our lives; I can hard-ly speak, I___
21
rall.
un - der-stand why you can't raise your voice to___ say...

Your Song

Words & Music by Elton John & Bernie Taupin

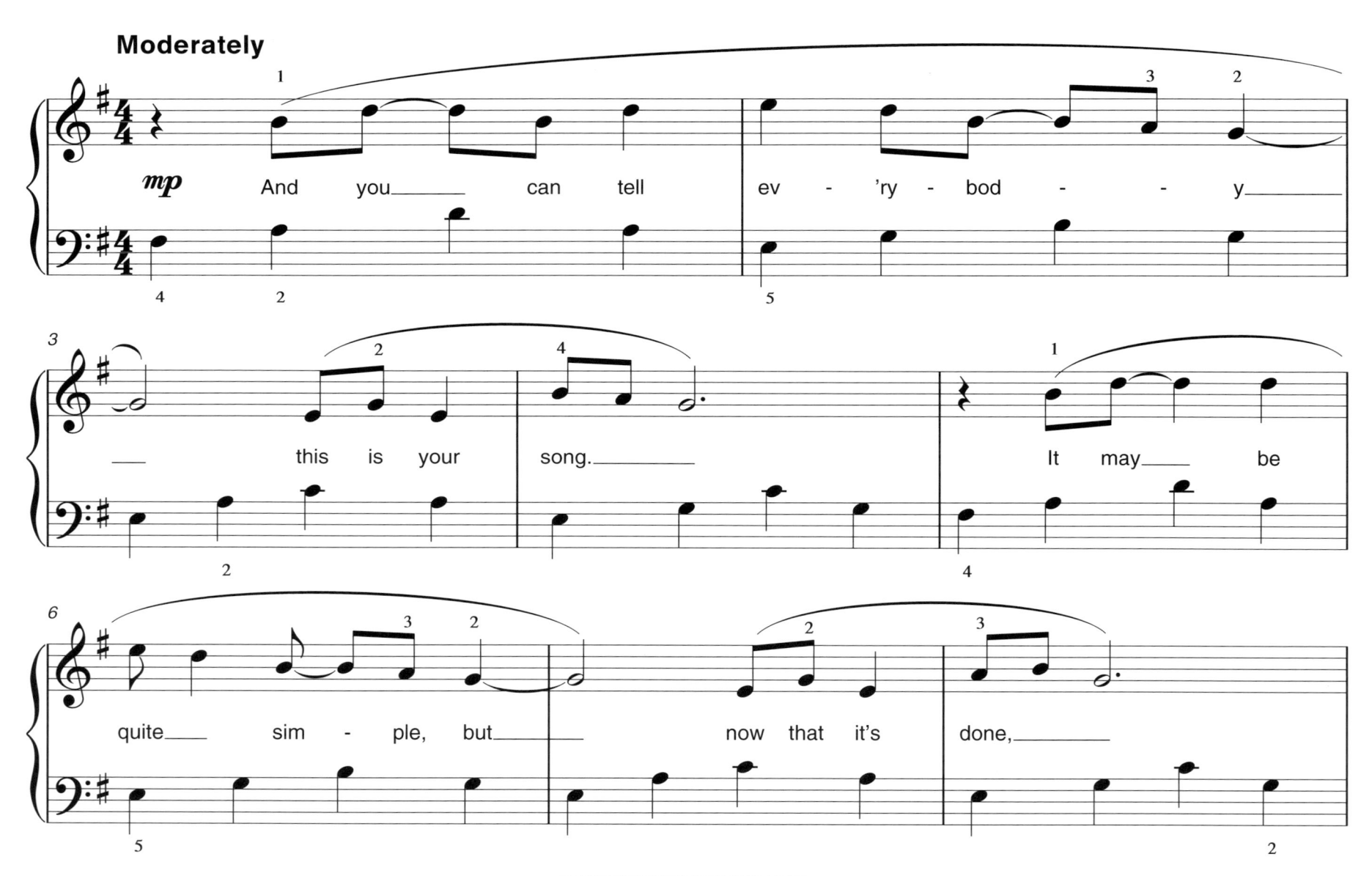

Moderately

And you can tell ev-'ry-bod-y this is your song. It may be quite sim-ple, but now that it's done,

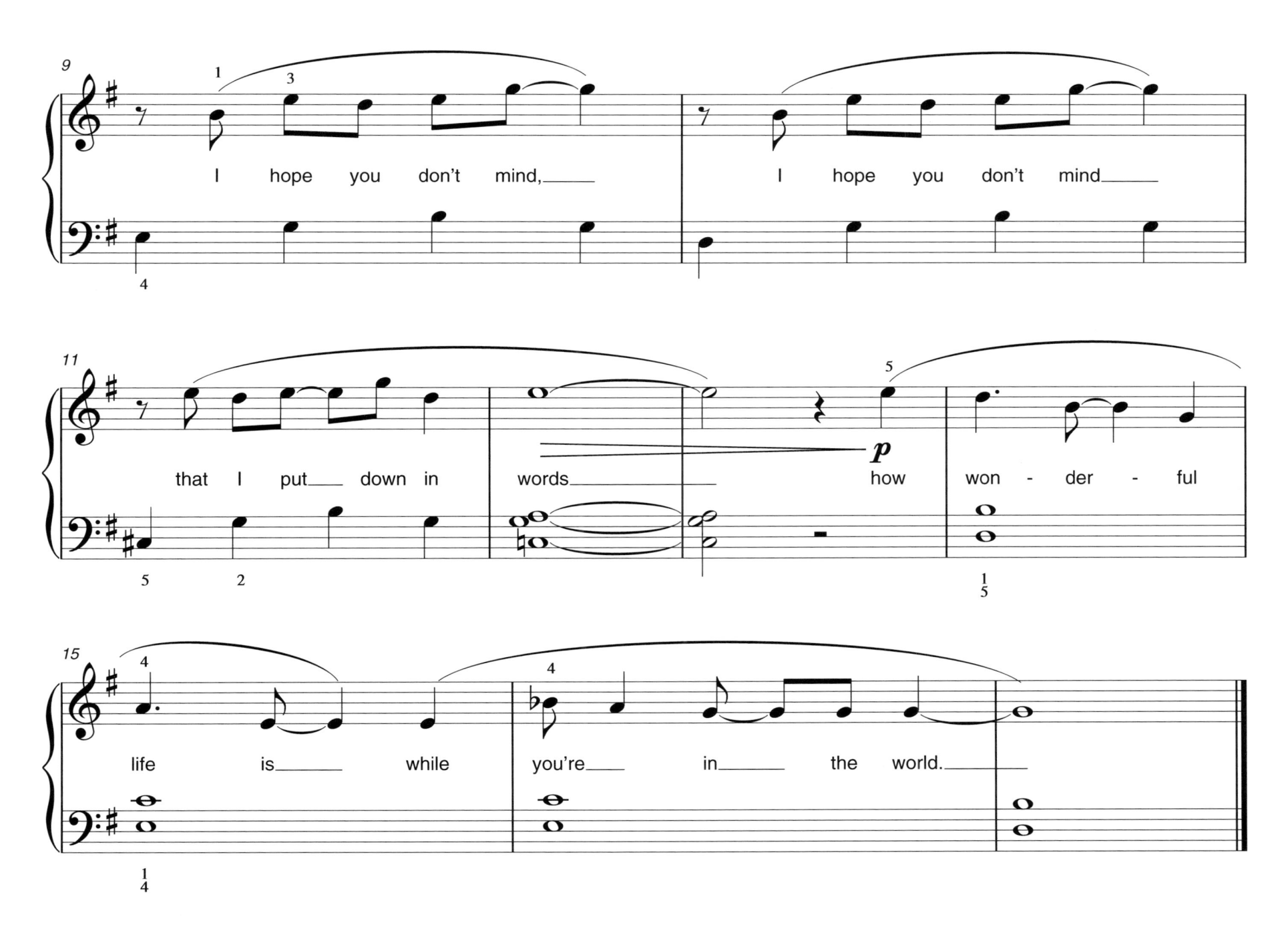

I hope you don't mind, I hope you don't mind that I put down in words how wonderful life is while you're in the world.

© Copyright 2013 The Willis Music Company
Florence, Kentucky, USA. All Rights Reserved.

Exclusive Distributors:
Music Sales Limited
Newmarket Road, Bury St Edmunds, Suffolk IP33 3YB, UK.
Music Sales Pty Limited
Units 3-4, 17 Willfox Street, Condell Park, NSW 2200, Australia.

Order No. WMR101288
ISBN: 978-1-78038-914-1

Unauthorised reproduction of any part of this publication by any means including photocopying is an infringement of copyright.

Arranged by Christopher Hussey.
Arrangements and engravings supplied by Camden Music Services.
Edited by Sam Lung.

Printed in the EU.